bed&bath
Decorating Ideas & Projects

Better Homes and Gardens® Books
Des Moines, Iowa

Better Homes and Gardens® Books
An imprint of Meredith® Books

***Bed & Bath* Decorating Ideas**
Editor: Linda Hallam
Art Director: Jerry J. Rank
Copy Chief: Catherine Hamrick
Copy and Production Editor: Terri Fredrickson
Book Production Managers: Pam Kvitne, Marjorie J. Schenkelberg
Contributing Copy Editor: Jennifer Mitchell
Contributing Proofreaders: Susie Kling, Beth Lastine, Jo Ellyn Witke
Contributing Photographers: Jenifer Jordan, King Au/Studio Au, Greg Scheideman
Indexer: Kathleen Poole
Electronic Production Coordinator: Paula Forest
Editorial and Design Assistants: Kaye Chabot, Mary Lee Gavin, Karen Schirm

Meredith® Books
Editor in Chief: James D. Blume
Design Director: Matt Strelecki
Managing Editor: Gregory H. Kayko
Executive Shelter Editor: Denise L. Caringer

Director, Retail Sales and Marketing: Terry Unsworth
Director, Sales, Special Markets: Rita McMullen
Director, Sales, Premiums: Michael A. Peterson
Director, Sales, Retail: Tom Wierzbicki
Director, Sales, Home & Garden Centers: Ray Wolf
Director, Book Marketing: Brad Elmitt
Director, Operations: George A. Susral
Director, Production: Douglas M. Johnston

Vice President, General Manager: Jamie L. Martin

***Better Homes and Gardens*® Magazine**
Editor in Chief: Jean LemMon
Executive Interior Design Editor: Sandra S. Soria

Meredith Publishing Group
President, Publishing Group: Christopher M. Little
Vice President, Consumer Marketing & Interactive Media: Hal Oringer

Meredith Corporation
Chairman and Chief Executive Officer: William T. Kerr

Chairman of the Executive Committee: E. T. Meredith III

Cover Photograph: Stephen Cridland. The room shown is on page 48.

All of us at Better Homes and Gardens® Books are dedicated to providing you with
information and ideas to enhance your home. We welcome your comments and
suggestions. Write to us at: Better Homes and Gardens® Books, Shelter Editorial
Department, 1716 Locust St., Des Moines, IA 50309-3023.

If you would like to purchase any of our books, check wherever quality books are sold.
Visit our website at bhg.com or bhgbooks.com.

contents

getting started

Bedrooms and baths are fun to decorate. They are our most private spaces, whimsical havens for our children, soothing retreats that welcome overnight guests. **Because they are so personal, bedrooms and baths lend themselves to creativity** in colors, fabrics, furnishings, and accessories. Unlike living and dining areas, **bedrooms can be tailored** to the ages, tastes, and needs of their occupants. In this book, you'll see hundreds of ideas and projects for master bedrooms, baths, children's rooms, and guest rooms. Turn to the chapters that interest you for inspiration and planning tips. **Selected, highlighted projects** throughout the book include detailed directions to help you accomplish your decorating goals.

As a **first step**, begin planning for **privacy, comfort, and safety** in both bedrooms and baths. As you look through each chapter, you'll see **ideas for window treatments** that address varying solutions for privacy and for children's safety. **Ideas for comfort** are found in all the featured projects, from chaise longues for reading and reclining to **tips for making the ultimate pampering bed.**

Whether you are planning to decorate all the bedrooms in your house or just a room or two, **consider needs, tastes, and individual desires.** If you have young children, your master bedroom may be the one room that allows you to **indulge in your favorite fabrics and furnishings.** If you need space for a hobby or a home office, tucking a desk in your own bedroom may be the **ideal answer** to a

space crunch. When your bedroom is just for you, **pamper yourself with the colors, furniture, and linens** you've always wanted. **Approach planning rooms** for children or overnight guests with the same eye to the personal. If your children are old enough, involve them in motif and color choices. For a nursery, consider **how the room will adapt** to your growing child. For guests, such adaptation may be the key. When space is at a premium, design a double-duty room that can serve as a home office or library and welcome guests. Or you may be able to carve out charming under-the-eaves spaces in a finished attic. **Planning and decorating ideas can translate from one room to another.** A color, fabric, or headboard in a guest room may inspire the decor in a master bedroom or child's room. Have **fun with ideas and projects** and use them as starting points to creativity. That's the **joy and satisfaction of home decorating!**

bedrooms

Surround yourself with your favorite colors, fabrics, or bed linens. This is your room—for you alone or to share with someone special. If you are starting from scratch, begin by choosing **your bed.** This one piece sets the style and mood of a bedroom—from soft and romantic to sleek and contemporary. **Emulate professional decorators** and **creatively mix and match** pieces. After selecting your bed, add side tables, a chest, and an armoire or wardrobe as you find them. If you like a unified look, collect mismatched pieces such as a bed frame and small tables and paint them white. **Introduce color** with bed linens.

When you have the luxury of a bedroom and bath suite, plan for the challenge of **decorating two spaces to work together.** As a quick starting point, **choose an appealing fabric** to inspire your color scheme. **Soothing floral patterns are classics.** For tailored or **contemporary styles, shop for stripes or a solid,** textured fabric or duvet cover. Choose a **color in your fabric to carry over to the walls** of one or all of the spaces. **Or paint one of your rooms in this color** and select a lighter or darker color from the same paint chip for other spaces. If you prefer wallpaper, start with a paper for the bedroom and pull out a pretty color for the bath. As a fabric option, choose a pattern that works well for bedroom draperies and for tailored Roman shades **that add privacy to the bath.**

masterbedrooms

Start with a fabric you love for your palette and decorating theme. Blue and white toile print turns this attic into a Parisian hideaway.

FABRIC INSPIRATIONS. Toile de Jouy, the classic scenic print, imparts an instant air of romance and ease. A favorite of designers because of its graphic quality, toile is most effective when repeated in lavish quantity and matching accents, such as lampshades.

◆ The toile inspired the headboard, which is hand-painted on the wall, *right*. To reinforce this carefully edited blue and white palette, the walls and ceiling are decoratively striped and painted in paler blues and creamy whites. Textured cotton slipcovers revived dated, basic bedside chests. **See pages 102–103 for project instructions.**

FABRIC INSPIRATIONS. For a relaxed touch, a toile slipcover imparts a stylish update to a thrift store chaise longue, *below left.* An old oval frame is revived with paint to set off a blue willow patterned plate. **See page 105 for project instructions.**

◆ Scraps of toile fabric cover the shades of swing-arm reading lamps, *below right.* Crisp, fresh sheets and fluffy pillow dress a bed with a chic new "headboard," hand-painted directly on the wall. **See page 102 for project instructions.**

◆ Toile is repeated in the bath, *opposite,* to visually tie the two adjoining spaces together. The fabric freshens a flea market vanity and mirror frame and puts a feminine twist on the director's chair. The shower curtain and window treatment are also decorative touches. Accessories in blue, white, and silver add a traditional feel. **See pages 104-105 for project instructions.** The deep blue in the toile fabric emphasizes the bathroom walls. A semigloss paint finish resists moisture, important for years of wear in a family bath. Pale blue towels and a white bath rug complete the easy, two-tone scheme.

MIX PAPER AND PAINT. Meet the challenge of existing bathroom tile with wallpaper, paint, and fabric. The secret of working with tile in an older bedroom and bath combination? Stay flexible with your color palette.

The wallpaper and stylized printed fabric echo the blue tile and introduce the shades of natural brown for transition to the bedroom palette, *left*. For textural interest, bedroom walls are decoratively ragged and glazed. This gives depth to a darker color so it doesn't overpower the room. A creamy shade of warm tan or papered walls in similar color variations would be equally effective and handsome design.

Pattern enlivens and warms this master bath with tile walls and mosaic-type tile floors, *above*. To create a focal point for the bath, the owners chose an oversize, novelty print shower curtain fabric in the spirit of the 1940s. With its stylized patterns and open background, the print also has a vaguely Oriental quality, which inspired the fanciful dragon motif and lattice wallpaper. The combination works because the colors are reinforced, but one pattern is clearly larger and more eye-catching. Note that the wallpaper appears as a repeating geometric for visual balance. Interest comes, too, from papering the ceiling for a finished and polished look in a chic setting.

INTRODUCE ORIENTAL. Influences from the Far East continue to thrive in decorating. Associated with pared-down decorating, this look translates with ease to bedrooms. Choose neutral backgrounds and add an Oriental-inspired piece to get started on your East-meets-West decor.

Repetition of strong shapes in bold furnishings, *above and opposite,* creates visual calm. Fewer, larger pieces and a minimum of small accessories, color, and pattern work with a tailored decorating approach. Concentrate on harmonious shapes and finishes, rather than periods or styles. The French-style metal bed and gilded chair are at home with an Eastern-influenced chest. Substituting the large mirror for a painting strengthens the setting without distracting color and scene. Shop for a large antique mirror or have a frame shop custom-make a similar mirror to different size specifications.

INTRODUCE ORIENTAL. A touch of the Far East adds texture to this spa-type bath. The background is clean and neutral with white fixtures, surfaces, and towels, *opposite*. Natural baskets and wood tones warm the setting.

◆ Incorporate a small, Oriental-style chest, *top right,* for extra bath storage and display. Shop at import stores that specialize in the Far East for a chest or carved trunk. Or purchase an unfinished chest with plain, straight lines. Stain it to a medium finish and add black and hand-painted details. Choose a piece compatible in shape and design with your bedroom furniture for a clean, unified look.

◆ Simplicity and serenity are the key elements for translating the spirit of the Orient into your bedroom and bath. Re-enamel an old clawfoot tub in sparkling, clean white for the deep soaks associated with Japanese bathhouses, *bottom right*. Include a small table, such as a metal patio table, that's easy to move. A simple vase provides a finishing touch.

ROMANCE AT RETAIL. Vintage pieces from antiques and thrift stores and estate sales add character and charm to this master bedroom, *above*. If you are lucky enough to find a pair of chairs and an ottoman, snatch them up for convivial bedroom seating. Or if older furnishings elude you, "age" new, reproduction pieces with crochet throws and pillows made from scraps of fabric and trim.

A mix of linens in muted colors makes the new metal bed look old, *opposite*. Choose fabrics that have a gently aged, tea-stained look (the effect of being soaked in a mild tea solution). To enhance the period ambience, introduce floral patterns in a mix of scales and patterns. For a pleasing, unified design, work with one common color, such as burgundy red, that repeats in the fabrics and rug. Instead of a larger painting, group a rack for straw hats and small botanical prints over the headboard. The effect is pleasingly personal without overpowering the old-fashioned scheme.

SIMPLIFY WITH BLACK AND WHITE. Toile de Jouy fabrics are one color printed over neutral backgrounds or the reverse, lending themselves to tailored applications appropriate to master bedrooms. When your goal is a bedroom that's sophisticated and not overly fussy, decorate with select touches of this French-inspired scenic print, *opposite*. For a no-fail scheme, use only colors in the toile, avoiding the distraction of competing colors.

In this bedroom, the soft white walls and black and white tweed carpet create a neutral backdrop for the traditional padded headboard and the more contemporary upholstered chairs and black lacquered bedside chests, *opposite*. This harmonious pairing of two different styles in a master bedroom, enlivened with the chic black accents of picture frames and linen details, creates a restful and comfortable retreat.

Take a tip from interior designers and repeat the shapes of furnishings for a sleek, well-planned look, *below*. The angled, straight lines of the chair back echo the bedside chest. Swing-arm lamps keep the bedside uncluttered and free for books.

CONTEMPORARY STARTING POINTS. Mid-century modern classics combine with a touch of the Oriental for a room beautiful in its spartan simplicity, *below*. Tables are made from lightweight, sandstone-colored planters.

◆ The headboard, inspired by a modern European classic design, replicates the warm tan wall color in a room with minimized contrast. **See page 107 for project instructions.**.

◆ In the adjoining sitting area, *below,* a bound sisal rug and operable shoji screens provide a serene backdrop with Oriental overtones. Rectangular, banded pillows and print neckroll pillows soften the contemporary sofa and chair. **See page 108 for project instructions.** Shop thrift stores and shops that specialize in 1950s and 1960s furniture for well-designed pieces. Edit accessories to just a few favorites.

◆ Maximize design impact with minimum pattern and repeated motifs. The picture frame reinforces the grid design of the woven headboard frame, *opposite below.* The straight, squared lines echo the contemporary coffee table, sofa, and chair in the adjoining sitting room. The round shape of the bedside table and torchère-style lamp provides a design counterpoint to the square window grids and headboard. The top of the table, a round piece of glass cut to fit, is painted in the same neutral shade as the urn to avoid visual distraction. Subdued linens warm with discreet pattern.

NEUTRALS PLUS COLOR. Neutral walls and flooring allow lots of options for a decorating direction. For impact, choose one strong color (*opposite*, the decor-setting cobalt blue) and one eye-catching pattern (the vibrant plaid) that set the scene. Stick with neutrals for fabric-heavy applications, such as the draperies, but add color with fabric-stingy treatments, such as the decorative valance and bench seat.

Paint small pieces, such as a table and chair, *below*, in a key color. Shop linen outlets and seasonal white sales for a mix of bright linens that amplify your current decorating theme.

NEUTRALS PLUS COLOR. Cobalt blue energizes and accents this bedroom, *opposite.* The second color from the lively palette (the bright green) adds a second accent. Colors from the plaid fabric reappear in accent pillows, throws, and accessories. If you prefer to keep your upholstery neutral, make colorful slipcovers for chairs.

◆ A coordinating geometric print repeats the blue of the bedroom in the adjoining bath, *above left,* and relaxes the starkness of an all-white, tiled bath. Carefully selected accessories add jolts of color.

◆ A mix of towels in vibrant hues carries the bedroom's decorating scheme into the bath, *above right.* Choose a white or off-white oversize bath rug to blend with tile. Or be bold and repeat a towel color.

◆ Bath accessories, *left,* in bright colors finish the scheme in upbeat style. Look for different sizes and shapes of bottles, dishes, bowls, vases, and candles for an interesting effect. Add soaps and a painted tray to keep everything neat and organized.

SUITE RELAXATION. Minimized color, pattern, and furnishings create a master suite that's serene and classic, *above left*. When working with multiple spaces and closets, choose paint colors, surface finishes, and details that unify. For areas such as closet halls and dressing rooms that receive little natural light, use the power of white to bounce light and to visually expand. Continue the carpet and flooring from area to area for a smooth flow. Bright touches, such as brass hardware, add sparkle to utilitarian, much-used spaces.

◆ Built-in storage, *above center,* takes advantage of small spaces for dressing room storage. As an alternative, shop for a small chest that fits your storage space and refresh it with white enamel paint and hardware. One unusual piece, such as a valet chair, personalizes the space.

◆ Durable, easy-care surfaces and color-coordinated fixtures reinterpret the palette for this bath, *above right*. A shelf provides an easy-to-change display. Inexpensive prints are perfect for a bathroom. Save prized art for the bedroom since even a well-ventilated bath is a damp environment.

◆ This suite's cool, pale, mint green wall color relaxes and updates traditional furniture, *opposite.* To give classic pieces a contemporary spin, simplify fabrics and pattern. Woven, textured patterns, such as the coverlet, bridge traditional and contemporary looks. To strengthen your scheme, repeat one of the fabrics. A pale gold is a classic, understated fabric for the camelback love seat and a handsome choice for the tailored Roman shades.

Bed & Bath **33**

ENRICH WITH VINTAGE FINDS. A touch of the well-worn sets the tone for a bedroom with old-fashioned charm no matter the age of the home. In today's personal decorating, the fun is in the mix of furniture and accessories. An old painted cabinet from the 1920s relaxes the look of a large-scale bed—and provides handy bedside storage, *opposite*. Experiment with shapes and finishes for accessories, too. The frame-over-frame effect of the small painting, collected photographs, and clock charm without undue clutter.

◆ When your goal is character and age, look for key pieces such as the well-worn rug and tufted chair, *below*, in soft, muted colors for your bedroom. You may find that the reverse side of a rug appears softer and more faded for a gently worn look. As you shop in antiques stores and thrift shops for finds to your liking, consider the well-made American and British pieces from the 1920s and 1930s. Although they are not yet considered to be true antiques, such pieces are prized for their strong lines, sturdy construction, and affordable prices. You'll also find art pottery from the early and mid-20th century, often with floral motifs, that contributes character and colorful accents.

UPDATE COTTAGE STYLE. Today's cleaned up cottage style creates relaxed room where soft color and charming furnishings take the place of undue clutter. Simple fabric shades speak to a lighter, cleaner look. Artless frames, painted to match the woodwork, pare down the decorating essentials, *opposite top and bottom left*. **See page 106 for project instructions.**

◆ Search for an interesting architectural fragment for a headboard that imparts style and character, *opposite top right*. Look for good design and shape; sturdy pieces can be cleaned, stripped, or repainted. **See page 106 for project instructions.**

◆ Balance the charm of a traditional cottage with cleaned-up contemporary. *below*. Choose one fabric pattern and repeat it to unify your scheme. Covering a lampshade in fabric gives a neat, finished look. Include a contemporary touch to lighten the scheme. This upholstered, Parsons-style bench fits perfectly at the window; a wicker trunk slides underneath for storage.

◆ Choose a variety of frame sizes and shapes for decorative interest, *opposite bottom left*. Hang a smaller frame inside a larger one for an interesting frame-within-a-frame effect. Remove the mirror to simplify a vintage dresser. Add a small box or covered dish to hold jewelry, coins, keys, or whatever finds its way to your dresser top.

◆ For design unity, choose a lamp base that echoes the material and color of the headboard. Here, the architectural shape of the lamp base, *opposite bottom right*, repeats the natural wood of the headboard in a contemporary, sleeker interpretation. Look for one-of-a-kind touches such as the shelf for tiny family photographs or a decorative alarm clock.

MELD CRAFTSMAN WITH CONTEMPORARY. Two of today's popular decorating trends, handcrafted Arts and Crafts and sleek contemporary, meet in this stylish bedroom. The two work well together as they feature strong shapes and a pared-down approach to decorating. The focal point is the contemporary flair of the Craftsman-style bed, *left*. The reproduction table lamps on metal bases are also the spirit of Arts and Crafts style. Nature-inspired browns, tans, creams, and greens soothe the senses and are appropriate to both styles. To emulate this look in your bedroom, start with the major furniture pieces. Base the color scheme—and the wall color—on the rug or upholstery. Hang a contemporary print or painting and your quiet retreat from the cluttered world is complete.

**MELD CRAFTSMAN WITH
CONTEMPORARY.** Natural
colors, wood, and leafy motifs
give an earthy spin to this
contemporary master bedroom.
Fresh white woodwork balances
the wall color and natural
woods. One motif—two versions
of leaves—visually relaxes
the setting while introducing a
subdued, sophisticated pattern.
Pinch-pleat draperies allow
the room to be flooded with light
during the day, yet close for
a cozy ambience in the evening.
The iron rod imparts a
Craftsman touch.

The bedroom's
soothing wall color continues
into the adjoining bath, *above*.
In the contemporary mood of
the space, finishes are sleek
and modern, and without
ornamentation. Black laminate
anchors the counter as a
sophisticated accent. Storage
baskets on open shelves
reinterpret the natural theme
of the bedroom.

Modern simplicity,
left, extends from the hall
into the master suite. Furniture
shapes and natural finishes
harmoniously link the spaces
for a comfortable transition.

COLORFUL QUILTS. A favorite quilt, hung as an instant headboard, sets a nostalgic mood in a modern bedroom. For an easy project like this one, *above,* purchase a drapery dowel rod with brackets at a home center or hardware store. Paint it white or an accent color that works with your quilt. Pull out a color from the quilt for your wall paint and use other quilt colors to paint a side table or chest. To avoid fading, don't expose a quilt to hours of direct sunlight.

A prized quilt gives this cozy library bedroom an even warmer feel, *left.* While it's fun to dress your bed in an heirloom vintage quilt, enjoy such fragile textiles with care. Immediately mend tears to avoid damage. And if you have a collection, rotate quilts for even wear. For regular everyday use, curl up under a sturdy new quilt. Add shams and pillows that match or contrast for read-in-bed comfort.

WARM WITH PADDED HEADBOARDS. A silk
fabric and tufted design create a mood of luxury and
sophistication, *above left*. Hang a lined bed hanging, and
a bedroom feels as sensual as a European villa. When
your decorating goal is an opulent air, work in shades of
gold, shell, pink, and amber. Check with a quality fabric
store for fine fabrics suitable for upholstered headboards.
Fabric stores are also sources of workrooms that make
custom headboards.

Prints and florals look best when stretched over
a padded headboard to show off pattern, using shirring
for detailing, *above*. When you find a fabric you adore,
enjoy it even more as a shirred headboard and matching
pillow shams. Tie the scheme together with a matching
bed skirt, shades, curtains, or lavish draperies.

One wonderful fabric does indeed make a
bedroom. For a professional appearance, choose a fabric
and headboard shape that are compatible in motif and
scale. The detailed arch of this headboard, *left*, calls for
a simplified, stylish pattern, such as this woven damask.
Nailheads give a neat, finished appearance. The tailored
bed skirt likewise reinforces the look and allows the
botanical pattern of the fabric to be clearly visible.

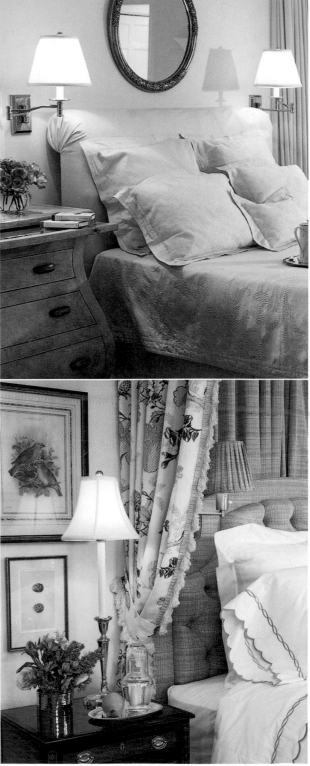

An exaggerated headboard shape pairs with a tailored scheme, *above*. Pattern and color are minimized, so the headboard stars without overpowering the room. Black welting neatly outlines and defines the shape. Add a second touch of this chic color with black shades for the standard, swing-arm lamps.

The gentle curves of a classic sleigh bed, *above right*, translate into an artfully curved headboard. Because the shape of the headboard is the strongest design element, choose a solid, woven fabric or a tone-on-tone fabric rather than a vibrant, busy print. (For an alternative, consider a two-color toile de Jouy.) Although traditional in its design origin, this version of the sleigh bed adapts well to contemporary or transitional decorating schemes because of its strong sculptural effect.

A neutral fabric works with interesting tufted details, *right*, for a classic look that's beautiful in a traditional setting. The fabric repeats as the lining for the floral bed hanging and as shades for swing-arm lamps. With a change of bed hangings, linens, and side chests, such a neutral headboard would work well in a more tailored setting. Silver accessories, including a lamp made from a candlestick, finish in elegant, traditional style.

bathrooms

Unleash your creativity to decorate this busy space. The bath is a perfect backdrop to experiment with your favorite colors and motifs. Depend on paint and easy-to-clean fabrics and finishes for a family-friendly environment. Because moisture can be a problem, make sure the room is well-ventilated with an exhaust fan and operable window. If the bath is part of a master suite, choose a lighter or darker hue of the bedroom color for your bath.

Be a little bold, but practical with color and pattern. You'll find medium color tones, such as apple green, sunny yellows, or sky blues don't show as much wear or scuffs as whites or dark shades. Look for your favorite paint color in a semigloss, scrubbable finish. If you prefer a pattern, use a stamp or stencil. Hand-paint stripes or a decorative finish on one or all walls. Paint the ceiling to match the walls. Or select a contrasting color or darker or lighter value of your wall color for the ceiling. To compensate for tight spaces, skirt your sink with hook-and-loop tape. Choose a cotton blend fabric that can be laundered frequently. Repeat the same fabric with a simple window valance or shade. Add stacked plastic storage bins or a large basket for convenient storage. Install extra towel bars on the wall, at child level if needed, and behind the door, to keep the room neat and tidy. Hang a fabric shower curtain with a plastic liner.

family bathrooms

Plan the bath as an extension of your home's style and color palette. Combine practical, durable finishes and fixtures with decorative details. Maximize handy storage, countertops, and lighting.

EMPHASIZE TEXTURES.
These mirrored walls reflect the rough-hewn granite sink, smooth marble countertop, and shiny brass hardware, *right.* Consult with a bath designer or showroom for fixtures such as this style-making bowl-style sink. As an alternative to stone, consider solid-surface materials or budget-stretching faux granite laminates. Drawers and shelves organize hidden under-the-counter storage. Plan for plenty of concealed storage to keep clutter at bay in such a sleek, contemporary setting.

UPDATE WITH PAINT. Painted beaded-board paneling and louvered shutters contribute a vintage look to this remodeled bath with a cheerful, pale yellow and bright white scheme, *above*. When space and budget allow, include details such as this inset tile "rug" that repeats the tile of the tub surround. The dark green tile visually balances the light walls and trim to anchor the room. Repeat the pleasing oval shape with a beveled mirror flanked by sconces. Dress up cabinets and drawers with cut-glass or ceramic pulls. Pay attention to the touches and details that enrich without breaking the budget. Shop home centers for affordable, reproduction pedestal sinks.

A summery color scheme of light sky blue and white, *above,* sets a beach-house mood for a budget-friendly decorating project. The homeowners painted dated paneling and drywall to match blue ceramic tile. Relax the look with accessories, such as hooks for towels, a wire basket, and a vintage, distressed table for bathside storage. White fixtures, window treatments, towels, bath rug, and accessories contribute to the fresh-air ambience. For the best painting results, prepare paneling to accept paint. Sand to remove any glossy finish. Or apply liquid sandpaper, a deglossing agent. Seal knots with shellac or clear lacquer. Let dry completely before priming with an alkyd primer tinted to your paint color.

UPDATE WITH FABRIC. Happy colors and a cheerful mix of fabrics energize this white tiled bath, *opposite.* For a lively transformation, the decorators replaced a standard issue medicine cabinet with a frankly fun mosaic mirror from a home furnishings shop. Next, they shopped for bright, washable, patterned fabrics to sew into a banded, gathered skirt for the vanity. (Hook-and-loop tape allows the skirt to be removed for laundering.) The space below hides plastic storage units and baskets for handy and accessible storage.

◆ Repeat fabrics and motifs for the window treatment, *left,* gives the bath a well-designed look. Here, the lighthearted, yellow-background print translates into a fixed window valance. Fabric-covered buttons, repeating a detail on the sink vanity, contribute a dressmaker touch. Blinds ensure privacy.

◆ A custom-made shower curtain dresses up a plain bath, *above.* A bullion-fringed trim, hand-sewn to a gathered valance, details. For interest, a geometric prints pairs with a cheerful botanical. Colors (two shades of green) repeat as the scale varies for pleasing visual balance.

ENLIVEN WITH COLOR. A permanent bath surface, tile is often used as a decorating starting point. Two or more colors of accent tiles easily mix with white for multiple design options. It's safest to match or blend wall color to one of the accent colors. In this bathroom, *above,* the wall color is upbeat pumpkin. Repeat the second tile color for a detail, such as trim and towels. If you prefer a white bath, paint only the trim in a tile color, and introduce vibrant accessories.

As a bold accent color, the painted bathroom door repeats one of the tile colors. In this easy-to-update scheme, a fresh coat of paint gives the bath a different decorating mood. As an alternative, choose black and white tiles for a chic, neutral backdrop. If you prefer, paint the door and trim white or off-white and choose your favorite tile color for the walls.

◆ Decorative tile gives design-savvy accents to this spa bath, *above*. You'll stretch your budget with this approach by minimizing the number of decorative tiles. And a clean, white scheme allows versatility in finishing details and accessories. For design interest, combine a variety of sizes of decorative tile for a mosaic, border effect. Include cove tile as a finished, decorative border. Enhance the sleek look with an opaque-glass door and a white porcelain knob.

◆ Minimize accessories and stash clutter to enjoy uncluttered simplicity, *right*. Enhance the simplicity with a tempered glass shelf on chrome brackets. Add wire or metal baskets or bins for sleek storage accessories. White towels and cotton bath mats are naturals in this spartan setting. For a brighter look, choose textiles that repeat one of the tile colors.

DECORATE WITH FLORALS. A pretty floral wallpaper turns a small bath tucked under the eaves into a romantic retreat, *left*. The open background and soft, serene colors create a soothing backdrop. The diamond pattern balances with its strong graphic. The floorcloth was painted to emulate the window treatment fabric. Shop for vintage pieces, such as the chest-turned-vanity and dressing table with a Gothic-style chair, that reflect the old-fashioned mood. An antique or painted reproduction cabinet adds charming storage for towels and soaps.

◆ A classic floral, such as the rose bouquet wallpaper, inspires this romantic style, *left*. Search antiques or thrift stores for nicely detailed mirrors and small tables or chests. If privacy isn't an issue, hang sheers or lace. Or combine sheers with blinds or shades for more privacy and sun control.

◆ A striped paper provides the harmonious background for floral fabric and art accents, *opposite*. For rooms with tall ceilings, add a chair rail and paint below in a blending, darker color. To imbue your room with instant glamour, hang an ornate vintage or reproduction mirror and dressy sconces with trimmed shades. A small corner étagère with space for extra guest towels and soaps contributes a gracious touch.

PERSONALIZE A POWDER ROOM. Rich, jewel box finishes and colors enliven this windowless interior space, *opposite*. Walls are papered with faux, leather-bound volumes for a library ambience; the ceiling and cabinets are darkened for drama. For such a nicely pulled-together look, choose colors from the wallpaper for the cabinet. (Here, the rich taupe.) Paint the ceiling a dramatic, deeper shade. Select semigloss paint to reflect light and include handsome accessories, such as a decorative shelf, crystal candlestick, or even a small chandelier.

◆ A handsome window treatment turns a standard window into the decorating focal point, *above left*. A decorative cornice combines with operable draperies and blinds for privacy. A small butler's tray on a stand adds storage and display.

◆ Spiffy striped wallpaper and an ornate sconce revive this small, dated powder room, *above right*. The single window is dressed with a lush Austrian shade. Touches of gilt and gold are incorporated with a framed print and decorative bracket.

◆ An elaborately framed mirror creates instant drama in a powder room, *right*. Look for reproduction mirrors in decorating catalogs and home accessories stores, or make the antiques store rounds to find the right prize. For a welcoming glow, pair it with torch-style sconces in parchment shades.

DRESS YOUR WINDOWS. A lighthearted window treatment and matching storage in this small bath turn the window into the design focus, *below left*. The tile, in two tints of pink, inspires the color scheme for the fabrics. For a lively look, the owner chose a geometric print for the fixed shade (hidden blinds provide privacy) and the upholstered window seat. A novelty print skirts the sink, reappears as one of the accent pillows on the window seat, and covers sconce shades. Towels monogrammed in pink, tassel trim, and gilt-frame prints demonstrate the decorating power of finishing touches.

◆ Utilitarian storage and a heating unit incorporate into a romantic window seat. The pale, subtle floral wallpaper and lacy sheers hint at pattern and color for a subdued, yet sophisticated scheme. For tailored balance, a crisp cotton check covers the window seat cushion; matching cording gives a neat finish. A detailed vintage frame and handsome pendant fixture add finishing touches for a pretty powder room.

◆ Taupe and white pair for a sophisticated, easy-to-emulate decorating scheme, *opposite*. This popular neutral look defines without overwhelming moderate-size spaces. For a twist on tradition, make a cornice from plywood and paint it in a faux fabric look. Paint and install louvered shutters below. For extra interest, decoratively paint or detail cabinet doors. If space allows, fill a planter or basket with moisture-loving plants.

SINKS AND MORE. A simple chest from a secondhand store converts into a vanity, *below*. Sand and prime before repainting furniture with a good-quality enamel. A self-rimming sink helps to keep water off the wood. For extra protection, seal the top of the chest with polyurethane. Detail with new ceramic hardware.

Upbeat surface colors and pattern energize a family-oriented bath with a practical double vanity, *below*. While white is a good, neutral choice for permanent laminates and porcelains, a busy room benefits from the cheerful look of colorful accent tiles, a mosaic back to open shelves, and checked wallpapers. Accent and trim

tiles enliven with color but allow change and versatility. In this bathroom, the checked paper and yellow accessories work well for young children and a casual look appropriate for a family. With a change of wallpaper or a decorative paint finish, the bath could take on a sleek contemporary or sporty seaside ambience.

◆ A lushly gathered skirt revives a vintage sink and adds concealed storage, *below*. A window treatment and a distressed bench complete the transformation. To make a skirt, measure the exposed rim of the sink and the rim to floor length. Triple the dimensions for a full look. For easy care, attach with hook-and-loop tape.

STORAGE WITH STYLE. For a handsome and practical chest-to-vanity conversion, convert a marble-top chest or washstand, *above*. The durable stone surface stands up well to family or guest use. Look for vintage pieces made in the late 19th and early 20th centuries, the heyday of the marble-top pieces. Or if you can't find the right chest or stand with marble, have a stone yard cut a piece to fit a sturdy, well-made chest. For a finishing detail, commission a finish carpenter to add a convenient towel rack on the side.

◆ A laundry bin pairs with open shelves to take advantage of tight space, *opposite top left*. For a neat look, buy towels in one or two colors and roll for storage. When space is extremely limited, attach a decorative hook for robes or towels.

◆ Flea markets, secondhand shops, and tag sales are sources for tall, narrow storage cabinets. Look for a well-made piece in a size that fits your space. Don't worry about color or hardware. For a clean look, repaint cabinets to match your wall color and/or trim. In a country- or cottage-style bath, add doilies or shelf trim, *opposite top right*. If your look is contemporary, shop vintage furniture stores for the medical supply, polished-metal cabinets. **Safety note:** Tall, narrow cabinets may not be stable. Such lightweight, easy-to-tip pieces aren't suitable in homes with young children.

◆ The pairing of louvered shutters and glass shelves recalls contemporary beach houses where clutter is artfully concealed and only decorative items are visible. Include space for a collection, *opposite bottom left*. Gravitate to fresh white backgrounds for a neutral backdrop. For a fun accent, purchase towel colors that repeat or blend with colors in your glass or pottery pieces.

◆ A balance of the contemporary and the traditional freshens this bath, *opposite bottom right*. Set the contemporary scene with clean white walls, open shelves, chrome fixtures, and a beveled, mirrored wall. Warm with a scrubbed pine table turned into a vanity. (Or apply clear matte polyurethane to an unfinished pine chest for a similar look.) Light with a pair of decorative candle sconces. For the most current decorating look, aim toward a pared-down look with necessities stored neatly out of sight. Create a chic, yet comfortable mood with lush white towels, white pottery, and crystal as easy-to-change accents.

guestrooms

Think of yourself as the visitor when you plan your guest room and bath. What do you need when you spend the night at an inn or a friend's home? Decorating and hospitality intertwine when you plan for family and friends. Don't be discouraged if you can't reserve a room for your visitors. Instead, add a futon, pull-down bed unit, or convertible sleeper sofa to your den, home office, or hobby room. Include a reading lamp, bedside table, lush bedding, extra pillows—and a water carafe at bedtime—for a comfortable, instant guest room.

When you do have a designated guest room, consider your visitors. Colors, such as pale pastels or soft neutrals, work well in guest rooms, soothing tired travelers. Padded headboards, too, set a tone of comfort and repose. When space is tight, small chests that double as nightstands and wall-mounted, swing-arm lamps are as stylish as they are practical.

Light-blocking window shades are also a good idea, especially if your guest room has an eastern exposure. Or choose a decorative window treatment that offers a degree of privacy. Think decoratively, too, when it comes to walls. Guest rooms are ideal canvases to try color combinations, specialty paint finishes, or a wallpaper you enjoy. And remember the extras, such as a telephone, small television, and clock radio, that say welcome.

Create a gracious getaway with comfortable furnishings, convenient storage, and well-appointed accessories. Choose soft, neutral colors and subtle patterns for relaxing serenity.

guestrooms

SITTING ROOM AS GUEST RETREAT. Planned and decorated as a handsome guest room, this retreat is also the owner's private sitting room between guests. The secret to such easy transition? An upholstered daybed that's equally enticing for overnight guests and daytime relaxing. Check out consignment shops for good buys on custom-made daybeds, or check with a fabric shop for a local custom workroom. For a sophisticated scheme, work in shades of beige, tan, taupe, and white. Choose a loop carpet or wool area rug for comfort, and update furniture with matching neutral linen or cotton slipcovers. Look for a beautiful mirror to pair with the chest. Include lamps for reading and mood lighting.

STUDIO TO GUEST SUITE. In this tucked-away retreat in a converted attic, guests enjoy the privacy often lacking in more conventional guest arrangements, *above left*. Consider your work or hobby studio for guest potential. For this double-duty option, start with a crisp white background and a cheerful palette. Group furniture to define function in an open space. The vintage desk works as a buffer between the sitting area, with facing blue and green sofas, and the worktable. If you need to maximize sleeping space, include a sleeper sofa or a pair of well made futons in the sitting area.

Follow these simple secrets, and you'll know how professional decorators successfully mix fabrics. Establish one color (*above center,* blue) that will anchor every fabric you use. The shades of your color don't have to match exactly but should blend. Choose at least one print and at least one stripe, check, or plaid. For more pattern, add on by finding a second print in a smaller or larger scale. To continue mixing, incorporate a second tailored fabric. If you chose a plaid first, include a check or stripe. To avoid a spotty look, repeat fabrics for pairs of chairs, window treatments, or accent pillows.

Turn a corner of a studio into a cozy nook for sleeping, *above right.* Dress a daybed with a dust ruffle and matching oversize pillows. Hide storage boxes with extra blankets and pillows underneath. This color-block print reinforces the room's green and blue scheme, yet also defines the sleeping area. The painted, color-block screen contributes to the weekend getaway mood of this enchanting space. So do the vintage accent tables, revived with fresh paint and whimsical detailing, too. Vintage reading lamps are freshened and updated with new white shades, trimmed for design interest.

LIBRARY WELCOMES GUEST. A built-in daybed, with concealed storage for linens and pillows beneath, turns an under-the-eaves corner into a guest room, *below*. For the most comfortable sleeping, purchase a firm mattress made for bunk or platform beds.

◆ Rich colors and paint finishes warm this sleeping nook, *opposite*. In a tight space, the designer included a wall-mounted sconce for guests who read in bed. For the ultimate cozy feeling, a lined drapery panel partially closes off the daybed. (Such an interior drapery panel, originally used to protect a bed or area of a room from drafts, is called a portiere.) To recreate this opulent look, which recalls 19th-century English gentlemen's libraries, include popular fabrics of that era, such as richly trimmed silk paisleys and geometric and stylized prints. Also incorporate the touches beloved by the well-traveled, erudite Victorians—faux animal skin prints, small oil paintings, fancy Venetian-style mirrors, and exotic rugs and tables. Check out import home furnishings stores that specialize in Africa, India, and Asia for tables, artifacts, and accessories.

MAKE ROOM FOR TRADITION. A black and white scheme provides a crisp, tailored background and works well as the canvas for sophisticated accessories. When you have space for a true guest room, savor the opportunity for creative decorating. The always popular and pretty toile de Jouy unifies and refines this decorating scheme, *left*. Since toile is effective in bold applications, choose a pattern that offers both wallpaper and matching fabric. Repeat the toile for the bed skirt and as slipcovers for upholstered pieces. Include black on painted furniture and as accessories to anchor the scheme. Update tables, chairs, and a chest with black enamel; include a lampshade.

Animate an old metal bed with a coat or two of white enamel, *above*. (For a smooth finish, sand and prime with a primer formulated for metal.) Paint a secondhand store side table to match and skirt the top for a playful accent. Dress the bed for summer in a ticking coverlet; warm the look in winter with a black and white plaid comforter or duvet. For a nicely designed look, resist straying from your two-color palette. Note the accent pillows decorated with motifs cut out from the toile. If blue is your color, you'll find toiles and ticking in shades that range from pale to dark. Or, consider the freshness of cool green toiles paired with stripes or the vibrancy of red toile and lighthearted checks.

OFFICE AS GUEST ROOM. A working home office welcomes guests with a modular system that includes a fold-down bed, *below*. **See page 112 for sources.** When you need to maximize space, look for units that include open shelving which doubles as side tables for guests, plus a desk and files. Well-designed units are sold in stained natural wood, painted, and laminate finishes.

Fold-down beds offer guests the comforts of a standard mattress because the mattress doesn't have to be pliable enough to fold. Double and twin sizes of fold-down bed units are available either as part of modular units as shown, *above,* or as frame units incorporated into custom-built cabinetry. As the bed is folded up and away, tucked-in linens can be left in place during the day. For decorating options, hang a print or poster above the bed. Or, if you are having custom cabinetry designed and installed, consider having narrow shelves built above or on the sides of the bed for necessities such as an alarm clock and reading lamp. As an alternative to the office location, have a fold-down bed installed between bookcases in a family or playroom. If you need more than one guest room during busy holiday times, one or more fold-down beds can be a cost-effective solution to a short-term space crunch.

COMFORTABLE CONVERTIBLES. The basic sofa anchors the living room and inspires the start of this guest room, *below left*. Buy a sleeper sofa the same way you do a mattress—try it out in the store. Unfold the bed and lie down. Test out several sofas in different quality ranges. In addition to construction, note the thickness and firmness of the mattress, which determines how comfortable the sofa will be. Choose other furnishings, such as the coffee table, that can be moved with ease if your sofa is in fairly frequent guest use. Include a small table and lamp for reading.

Splurge on a set of decorative cotton sheets, and sleeping on the sofa will be a treat, *above right*. Remember the basics and cover the mattress with a thick, quilted pad before making the bed. Guests appreciate an extra blanket, oversize pillows for reading and relaxing, and a soft coverlet or throw, too. **See page 111 for ideas to make the ultimate luxurious bed.**

When you occasionally need an extra bed but not an extra bedroom, include a sleek daybed like this one, *opposite*, in a sitting room—or even a corner of your dining room. You'll enjoy the daybed for sitting and relaxing and as a handsome addition to your decor. When your home is overflowing with guests, you'll have one more comfortable single bed. To shop for an upholstered daybed, search consignment shops that deal with estate sales. Although the fabric may need to be replaced to work with your scheme, a secondhand daybed is likely to be structurally sound. *Alternatives:* reproduction wicker, wood frame, or metal daybeds from import or furniture stores.

kids'rooms

Color, color, color. Whether the room is for a boy or girl, teen or infant, **color is the strongest direction in decorating.** Fortunately, it is the **quickest, easiest, and most budget-conscious,** too. For nurseries, pastels never go out of style, but **the current trend** is brighter, more vibrant shades of the traditional blue, pink, yellow, and green. **For a quick start,** shop for fabric or a wallpaper border in happy colors. **Or paint the walls in a lively color and stencil or stamp a motif** as a chair rail, around a window, or as the ceiling border. **Stretch your nursery budget with carefully selected used or unpainted furniture.** (Make sure any older crib meets safety requirements, with slats no more than 2⅜ inches apart.) Paint the crib, chest, changing table, and rocking chair with white enamel or your favorite color and add stamped, stenciled, or hand-painted decorative touches.

When you are **decorating for a school-age child or a teen,** consider his or her interests—geography, science, sports, animals, dance—to come up with a theme and color scheme. Look at fabrics or wallpaper borders for inspiration. Always **incorporate study and storage areas** into the planning mix. **For a quick start,** purchase unfinished **storage cubes or small bookcases,** add a plywood top and paint them color-block style, in three bright colors. **Look for bargain finds,** such as old-fashioned wooden folding chairs, that can be painted to match.

kids'rooms

Create a haven for your child with a vibrant decorating theme that encourages flights of imagination.

COLOR THEIR WORLD. A fantasy bed and Toucan bird novelty print fabric inspire an explore-the-world theme, *right*. With time, paint, and maps for reference, such elements turn a child's room into a daily geography lesson. As a starting point, an exotic, novelty print fabric sets the color palette; pulled-out colors translate into the striped walls, painted first for the backdrop. A decorative painter used maps as references; then sketched and painted stylized maps across the ceiling and down the striped wall. Varied colors of countries, the same palette, lend an exuberant tone. If you are looking for a decorative painter for such a project, consider a talented college art student or high school or college art instructor.

TOPIARIES FOR TWO. Two complementary fabrics, a floral stripe and a floral diamond, are designed to be used together as a no-fail decorating short cut in this girl's bedroom, *below*. The pairing of spring-fresh green balances the sweetness of traditional pale pink and naturally welcomes garden-style decorating. In this room, shared by sisters, the color scheme naturally translates to the topiaries, handpainted by a local artist on the doors of a painted armoire.

This awning style, with bead trim and plaid shade, *opposite top left*, is tailored enough to work into the teen years. Local fabric shops can suggest workrooms that craft such stylish treatments.

Paint and a garden-fresh design turned a basic armoire into a decorating focal point, *opposite top right*. The handpainted borders framing the topiaries and the painted detailing contribute to the charm.

Two of the fabrics repeat for a gathered table skirt, sewn with cording and a border, *opposite bottom left*. A plaid pattern balances a more decorative floral while reinforcing the spring-fresh, pink and green scheme.

A harlequin pattern is an ideal choice for spreads with flirty skirts, *opposite bottom right*. For the nicest hang, the seamstress chose a lightweight cotton fabric, gathered with cording to the coverlet top. Delicate, stylized flowers in the fabric colors are handpainted over the distressed finish of the bedposts. Touches of blue accent the bedpost trim.

PAINT THE SCENE. Who needs a headboard for an appealing bedroom? In this bedroom, loosely painted stylized flowers and swirls are based on the decorating fabrics, *below left*. This technique works best if you dip a large, tapered artist's brush or small paintbrush into latex paint and quickly paint the scene. For confidence, practice first on a large piece of poster board. Experiment with diluting paint with glaze for the look of delicate watercolors. With a colored pencil, mark guide points where you'll paint in the flowers and the swirls.

This attic room takes young space explorers where they have never gone before with a space shuttle aimed at moon and planets, *above*. Mom hand-painted worlds beyond with latex and artist paints. If you prefer a quick project, add glow-in-the-dark stars and wallpaper cutouts or decal motifs. Dress the bed with stripes and an American flag pillow.

Beachcombers will enjoy a never-ending summer vacation in this room based on sun and sand, *opposite*. To achieve the look, collect pieces of driftwood to attach to a bed frame and craft into a small table. Hang a wooden fishing pole to hold a gauzy window treatment. Add a chair rail and paint or wallpaper the sea and sky above. (If you paint, sponge on fluffy clouds.) Paint the sand below and choose a durable natural-colored carpet.

GENDER-NEUTRAL NURSERY.

This bright pastel nursery awaits either a boy or a girl with a lively color palette, *left*. The painted striped walls and stenciled gingham border are combined for lighthearted fun. **See pages 109–110 for project instructions.**

The gingham stencil motif repeats on the window cornice, *opposite*. Ready-made sheers soften the look and shades or blinds offer privacy and sun control. Stretch your budget by repainting a secondhand crib with fresh white paint. If you are using an older crib, be sure it meets current safety standards—slats no more than 2⅜ inches apart. **See pages 109–110 for project instructions.** Soft flannel fabrics in bright pastels adorn ready-made cushions and pillows. An old garden bench painted white matches the crib and import-store wicker rockers. A crisp yellow and white checked bumper pad and dust ruffle dress the crib. A yellow rug is a vibrant accent to tie the decorating scheme together, *below*. **See pages 109–110 for project instructions.**

Make a plywood cornice or work with a local woodworking shop to recreate a decorative design, *right*. Repeat the gingham stencil with matching colors to unify your lighthearted project. **See pages 109–110 for project instructions.**

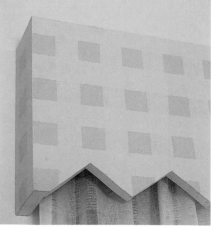

GROW UP IN AN ANIMAL KINGDOM. Two styles of a novelty print fabric, plus a complementary plaid, give a tailored look appropriate now for stuffed bears—and later for sports motifs and gear, *left*. Quality fabrics and well-made furniture move from toddler times into elementary school years. In a home with traditional decor, the designer worked with classic fabrics and furniture and accessories that gracefully span the years. The sporty blue and white color scheme is based on detailed 19th-century prints and illustrations popular in England and America. For instant art, the plaid is framed as the canvas for handprints.

◆ This animal print, *above,* is ideal for a motif that's youthful, but not babyish or overly cute or trendy. Plaids, too, transcend the years for a boy's room. The reproduction Staffordshire Highlander lamp is in the Scottish theme that works well with plaids, based on the tartans of the Highland clans. When the young gentleman tires of animals, the shams can be replaced with red and blue pillow covers.

◆ In rooms with a mix of window styles, such as this upstairs space, a lively fabric works with two styles, such as the cornice and draperies, *right*, and the Roman shade, *left*. The animals energize the cobalt blue walls and give a theme to the room. And the shape of the cornice recalls castles—reinforcing the Scottish theme.

DAYBEDS/SLEIGH BEDS. A garden-bench style bed with graceful curves evokes French style, *above left*. Bows, ruffles, and swags inspire delicately painted wall accents. A gathered shade and a mix of pillow shapes with ruffles and bows contribute girlish accents.

◆ Crayon colors energize a small room, *above right*. To emulate the look, paint a bed in primary blue and yellow and add a fun '60s touch with a "flower power" rug. Stretch your budget by painting the walls in a cheerful hue and detailing them with an easy-to-hang wallpaper border.

◆ Encourage the artist in your child with a bed you paint together with swirls and brush strokes, *left*. Paint a storage cube or small chest to match. Ask your child to paint his or her own masterpiece, then paint a colorful, fanciful frame to go around it.

◆ Design a bedroom regal enough for a little princess with an antique daybed and a hand-painted (or wallpapered) background that recalls the fanciful illustrations of classic children's literature, *opposite*. Warm with an old-fashioned floral carpet and dress the windows, under a cornice, with wisps of translucent sheers.

decoratingideas

bed & bath projects

HAND-PAINTED HEADBOARD
SKILL LEVEL
Intermediate
TIME (NOT INCLUDING PAINTING BASE COAT)
1 day
SUPPLIES
- Artist's pencils
- Brown kraft paper or brown paper drop cloth
- Tape measure
- Scissors
- Tape
- Straight edge ruler
- Paint in your color choices
- Small, tapered artist's brushes

HAND-PAINTED HEADBOARD
(PICTURED ON PAGES 12–14)

■ **A painted headboard is an ideal solution for** attic-type rooms without space for a conventional headboard. Depending on your skill and style, the headboard can be as elaborate or as simple as you like. The focal point for this headboard was copied from the room's decorating fabric.

■ **Decide what size and style headboard you want.** If the ceiling is low and sloped, as in a converted attic, leave at least 2 inches between the top of the headboard and the slope to avoid a jammed look. For the sides, consider an extra 5 inches on each side of the bed so the headboard is visible. Before you start, place the bed, made up with all the bedding you plan to use, against the wall. Use a pencil to mark how wide you want the headboard to be.

■ **After you have a rough idea of the size of the headboard**, make the pattern from brown kraft paper or a brown paper drop cloth. Measure the wall with a tape measure. Using those measurements, cut a large rectangle from the paper, approximately the size of the headboard. Tape the paper headboard to the wall to make sure the width and height look right. Adjust the size of the pattern as needed. With a pencil, mark the pattern at the middle. Mark the sides of the pattern. Draw the top curve of the headboard pattern for the style shown here. Or draw the style you prefer. Draw half of the pattern. Remove the pattern, fold in half, and cut out. Unfold and tape in place again. Trace with a pencil. Use a ruler to help with straight edges if necessary. Move the

bed away from the wall.

■ **Hand-paint the background color in your choice of latex paint** (here, dark blue). You don't have to go all the way to the floor because the mattress will cover up the dead space. Simply draw a straight line across the bottom of the main part of the headboard. (The line can be loosely drawn as it won't show.) Allow the base coat to dry. Loosely brush on a top coat of cream-colored latex paint. Use small, tapered artist's brushes for more detailed areas. Allow to dry. Add hand-painted details to the spindles, posts, or other features of your headboard. This headboard has darker detailing, with lighter highlights painted on top.

■ **If you aren't comfortable painting freehand,** use a commercial headboard stencil, available through stencil catalogs. Or design your own headboard with a combination of stencils and/or stamps. Be creative—you can paint over any mistakes.

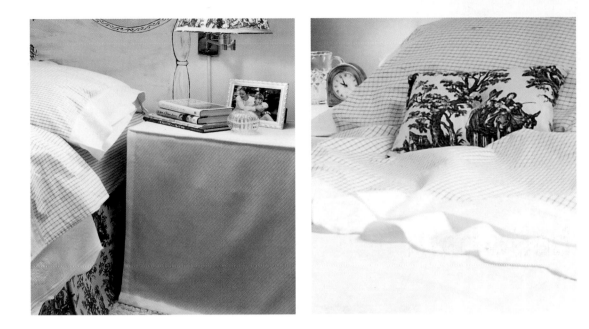

SLIPCOVERED BEDSIDE TABLE
SKILL LEVEL
Advanced
TIME
4 to 5 hours
SUPPLIES
- Tracing paper
- Pencil
- Medium-weight fabric (yardage based on table size)
- Cording (enough to go around top of table, plus several inches)
- Matching thread
- Tape measure
- Straight pins

BUTTON PILLOW SHAM
SKILL LEVEL
Intermediate
TIME
2 hours
SUPPLIES
- Fabric
- Thread
- 14-inch pillow form
- Covered button kit
- Tape measure
- Straight pins

SLIPCOVERED BEDSIDE TABLE
(PICTURED ON PAGES 12–13)
- **For the slipcover,** you'll need patterns for one top, two sides, one back band, and one front flap. Measure the table and make patterns from tracing paper as follows:
- **For the top,** measure the top of the table and add ½-inch seam allowances to all four sides. For the sides, measure the depth of the table (front to back) and the length (top edge of the table to the floor). Add 2½ inches to the depth measurement (½ inch for hems and 1½ inches to wrap around the front) and 2½ inches to the length (½ inch for the seam and 2 inches for the hem). For the back band, make a pattern that measures 4½ inches tall (includes a ½-inch seam allowance and 1-inch hems) by the width of the table plus 1 inch (for ½-inch side seam allowances). For the front flap, make a pattern that measures the width of the table plus 4 inches (for 2-inch hems) by the length (top edge of the table to the floor) plus 2½ inches (½ inch for the seam allowance and 2 inches for hem).
- **Cut the top,** two sides, one back band, and one front flap from the fabric. From the remaining fabric, cut 2-inch-wide fabric strips on the diagonal. Piece the strips together until they make a strip long enough to cover the cording. Fold the strip in half with wrong sides facing and the cording in between. Stitch in place. Using ½-inch seam allowances, sew the cording around the top fabric piece.
- **Hem the fabric pieces as follows:** Press under ½-inch on each side of the side pieces and stitch.

Press under 1 inch twice on each side of the front flap and stitch. Press under 1 inch twice to hem the two side pieces and the bottom of the front flap. Stitch in place. Press under 1 inch on the bottom edge of the back band and stitch.
- **Pin the pieces together for the final stitching.** Lay top piece flat with right side up. Pin raw edge of the back band to the back edge of the top piece. Pin side pieces to the sides of the top, bending 1½ inches to overlap on the front edge of the top. Lay the front flap over the top of the last open edge and pin in place. Stitch the pieces together. Turn and press.

BUTTON PILLOW SHAM
(PICTURED ON PAGES 12–14)
- **Measure the pillow form,** cut two fabric shapes to the measurements of the pillow, plus ½ inch all around for seam allowances. With right sides facing, sew the fabric shapes together, leaving one side unstitched so you can insert the pillow form. Clip the corners, turn right side out, and press. Insert the pillow form and slip-stitch the opening closed. Follow instructions on package to cover large center button. To apply button, locate the center with a long needle and heavy thread. Knot off thread on the back side with a plain clear button. Stitch through the front of the pillow; string the covered button onto the needle. Push the needle back down through the center until it is threaded through the back button. Do this several times, being sure the thread is tight. Knot off the thread by winding the thread around the back button. Make a tailor's knot.

DIRECTOR'S CHAIR COVERS
SKILL LEVEL
Intermediate
TIME
3 to 4 hours
SUPPLIES
- Fabric
- Thread
- Tape measure
- Straight pins

FABRIC-COVERED MIRROR
SKILL LEVEL
Intermediate
TIME (NOT INCLUDING DRYING TIME)
2 hours
SUPPLIES
- Frame
- Mirror cut to fit
- Fabric
- White latex paint
- Aerosol fabric protector
- Spray adhesive
- Cardboard
- Glazing points
- Screw eyes
- Picture wire

DIRECTOR'S CHAIR COVERS
(PICTURED ON PAGE 15)

- **For the body of the slipcover**, measure from the floor at the back of the chair, up over the back and across the seat. Measure to the floor on the front of the chair. (If you are working with a patterned fabric, such as the toile featured here, plan for a seam at the top back of the chair so the pattern isn't upside down.) Measure the width from side to side. Add 1 inch on all edges for seams and hems.

- **For sides**, measure from the seat up across the arm and down to the floor. Measure the width from front of arm to back of arm. Add 1 inch on all edges for seams and hems.

- **Stitch double** ½-inch hems on long sides of side pieces.

- **Lay the body piece on the chair**, centered front to back and side to side. Pin side pieces to body so they align with chair arm. Stitch into place. Hem all edges of the body and remaining short edges on each side piece.

- **For ties, cut eight strips**, each measuring 1×18 inches. For each strip, press under ¼ inch at the short ends. With the wrong sides facing, press the long raw edges to meet in the center of the strip. Fold strip in half lengthwise, encasing the raw edges. Stitch in place.

- **Reapply cover to the chair** and align for ties. Mark placement for ties with pencil or pen and stitch in place.

FABRIC-COVERED MIRROR
(PICTURED ON PAGE 15)

- **Purchase a flat frame without decorative elements**. This allows for the easiest application of fabric. Choose a frame wide enough to show any pattern, especially if you are using a fabric such as the scenic toile shown here. Paint the frame white for an even, solid background for your fabric. Allow to dry thoroughly.

- **Before you begin working with the frame**, make sure your hands are clean since any dirt or grime will be transferred to the fabric from the handling. (Spray the fabric with an aerosol fabric protector either before or after you apply it to the frame.) Lay fabric over the frame to establish where the pattern will be placed if using a patterned fabric. Cut the fabric several inches larger than the frame to allow it to be adhered to the backside of the frame. Spray the front of the frame with spray adhesive. Position fabric, press and smooth into place. Wrap the sides around back and glue in place with fabric adhesive.

- **Cut fabric from the opening** of the frame so that the opening in the fabric is several inches smaller than that of the frame. At each of the four corners, make a diagonal cut from the corner of the opening in the fabric to the corner of the inside of the frame. Wrap and glue each side to the backside of the frame. Cut a cardboard backing the same size as the mirror. Fit the mirror and backing into the frame using glazing points from a hardware store. Add screw eyes one-third of the way down the back of the frame, attach wire and hang.

ANTIQUED PICTURE FRAME WITH FABRIC-COVERED HANGER

SKILL LEVEL
Beginner

TIME (NOT INCLUDING DRYING TIME)
2 to 3 hours

SUPPLIES

- Large, paintable oval frame
- White or cream artist's acrylic paint
- Crackling medium
- Accent color of artist's acrylic paint
- Small artist's brushes
- Picture wire
- Picture hanger
- Fabric
- Plate or framed art

TABBED SHOWER CURTAIN

SKILL LEVEL
Intermediate

TIME
1 day

SUPPLIES

- Fabric
- Thread
- Tape measure
- Straight pins
- Buttons

ANTIQUED PICTURE FRAME WITH FABRIC-COVERED HANGER
(PICTURED ON PAGES 12, 14)

■ **Choose a decorative frame that can be painted**. Paint with a base coat of artist's acrylic paint. Apply the crackling medium according to the directions on the bottle. Highlight decorative details with the accent paint by brushing darker paint into low-relief areas and wiping paint away from areas to be highlighted. Allow the frame to dry. Attach a picture wire behind the frame to determine the length of wire to be used. Detach one end of wire from frame. Make a fabric sleeve from 2 yards of a 3-inch-wide strip of your decorating fabric. Fold the strip in half lengthwise with right sides facing. Sew the long edge with a ¼-inch seam. Turn and gather on the wire. Attach loose end of the wire to the back of the frame. Attach a plate hanger to your plate and hang centered in picture frame.

TABBED SHOWER CURTAIN
(PICTURED ON PAGE 15)

■ **Measure the curtain length from the top of the rod** to the floor. Plan the width (the standard is 72 inches finished) and add 8 inches. Cut two 45-inch-wide pieces of fabric to the determined length, plus 4 inches. Decide on the number of tabs for your curtain. Cut each tab to measure 5×9 inches. Fold each tab lengthwise with right sides facing. Sew tab with a ¼-inch seam, tapering stitching to a point at one end. Leave the other end open for turning. Trim tapered end, turn, and press. Stitch a lengthwise buttonhole on each pointed end.

■ **Seam the two fabric lengths together**. Press. Recut to 80 inches wide. Hem sides with double 2-inch hems. Press top with ½ plus 1½ inch hem. Pin into place. Align cut edge of tabs across top of curtain, placing one on each end and one at the center. Space remaining tabs evenly across curtain. Stitch with two rows of stitching, one at the top edge to catch the tabs and the other along the lower edge of the top curtain hem.

■ **Hem the lower edge of the curtain** with a double 2-inch hem. Fold tabs to the front of the curtain and mark spots for buttons through the buttonholes. Stitch buttons in place. Hang with a liner from a shower rod.

PAINTED PICTURE FRAMES
SKILL LEVEL
Beginner
TIME (NOT INCLUDING DRYING TIME)
3 to 4 hours
SUPPLIES
- Frames in various shapes and sizes
- Paint in your color choice
- Small brushes
- Paper
- Tape
- Small nails

FRAGMENT HEADBOARD
SKILL LEVEL
Beginner
TIME (NOT INCLUDING STRIPPING TIME)
1 hour
SUPPLIES
- Fragment
- Stripping medium or paint supplies as needed
- Soft lead pencil
- Heavy-duty picture hangers

PAINTED PICTURE FRAMES
(PICTURED ON PAGES 36–37)
- **Collect a variety of paintable picture frames** in assorted shapes and sizes. Economical sources include discount stores, garage and tag sales, thrift stores, and consignment shops. Collect more frames than you think you'll need. Scale and shape are more important than finish since you will be painting the frames all one color. Select a color for your frames. For this project, an assortment of frames was painted in a satin latex paint that matches the woodwork.
- **To make an arrangement with your frames,** cut paper silhouettes of the frames and attach the cutouts to the wall with small pieces of tape. They can be moved easily to establish a pleasing composition. Even space between frames and balanced arrangements is visually appealing. Use a small finishing nail to hang each frame. If you change your mind or need to adjust the heights of the frames, you'll only have small holes to fill and touch up. When you are satisfied with the arrangement, use a small level and hang each frame on two nails. This balance makes the frames more secure and less likely to move.

FRAGMENT HEADBOARD
(PICTURED ON PAGE 36)
- **Consignment and secondhand shops are ideal** places to search for fragments that can be converted into headboards. For this project, the headboard was an antique mirror and frame from a chest of drawers. If the original finish doesn't work with your room, strip or paint it as needed. In this example, the wood was stripped with a commercial stripper to reveal the light oak.
- **To hang a headboard fragment,** enlist help. One person (or two if the fragment is very heavy) should hold the fragment against the wall while the other determines how level it is. Mark with a soft lead pencil where you will hang the headboard on each end. Use two heavy-duty picture hangers to hang securely in place. Mirror frames from old dressers, wooden architectural elements, metal grates, and old gates make interesting, handsome headboards. Make sure any element you use is securely attached to the wall with heavy-duty hangers.

WOVEN HEADBOARD
SKILL LEVEL
Intermediate
TIME (NOT INCLUDING
FRAME CONSTRUCTION)
4 hours
SUPPLIES
- Frame constructed from
1×4s, 2 at 55 inches
and 2 at 36 inches
- Fabric scraps for
practice and measuring
- 3-inch-wide elastic
upholstery banding
(approximately 20 yards
for the queen-size bed
in this example)
- Staple gun with
heavy-duty staples
- Heavy-duty picture hangers
- Level
- Soft lead pencil

URN SIDE TABLES
SKILL LEVEL
Beginner
TIME (WITH DRYING TIME)
2 hours
SUPPLIES
- Imitation stone urns
with an interior lip
- Glass rounds custom-cut
- Latex paint to match urn
- Small paint brush

WOVEN HEADBOARD
(PICTURED ON PAGE **26**)
- **Determine the size of your headboard** width
and height to fit your bed frame. For this
example, a woodworking shop constructed the
frame from 1×4s joined with a biscuit joiner.
However, metal "L" brackets could also be used.
To avoid wasting elastic banding, cut strips of
fabric from inexpensive cotton and practice
weaving your headboard as shown. In this
example, the horizontal strips were stretched and
stapled into place before the vertical banding was
woven. Measure the strips to determine how
much banding is required for an attractive woven
headboard. Add an extra yard to make sure you
have sufficient banding. Weave banding strips
and staple into place.
- **With the aid of a helper,** hold the headboard
in place. Straighten with a level and mark where
you'll hang the headboard. Attach to the wall
with heavy-duty picture hangers on each end of
the headboard.
- **Elastic banding source:** The elastic banding
used in this project was ordered from
King Textiles, Inc., 44 Richmond St. West,
Toronto, Ontario, Canada; 416/504-0600.

URN SIDE TABLES
(PICTURED ON PAGE **26**)
- **Select lightweight imitation stone urns** in a
comfortable bedside height. Be sure the urns
you choose have an inner lip to hold the glass in
place. Have glass rounds cut to fit inside the urn.
Paint the underside of the glass the same color
as the urn (here, a sandstone color). Allow to dry.
Set the glass in the urn for an attractive and
quick table.
- **Urn source:** The urns for this project were
ordered from American Designer Pottery, 13612
Midway Rd., Suite 200, Dallas, Texas 75244;
888/388-0319; wwwamdesignerpottery.com.

SHOJI-STYLE SLIDING SCREENS
SKILL LEVEL
Advanced
TIME (NOT INCLUDING FRAME CONSTRUCTION)
1 to 2 days
SUPPLIES
- Lightweight frames constructed from 1×¾-inch poplar wood
- Vellum paper from an art supply store
- Household glue
- Sliding door tracks and hardware
- 1-inch wood screws

FABRIC-STRIPED PILLOWS
SKILL LEVEL
Beginner
TIME
1 to 2 hours
SUPPLIES
- Two contrasting color fabrics
- Thin batting material
- Thread
- Fiberfill or pillow form

SHOJI-STYLE SLIDING SCREENS
(PICTURED ON PAGES 26–27)
- **Shoji screens are most effective in rooms with walls of windows or large windows** as their beauty comes from the soft, diffused light. They provide privacy without blocking light.
- **For this project,** a woodworking shop constructed the lightweight frames from poplar wood and finishing nails. Dimensions were based on the sizes of the windows. Use vellum paper larger than the frame. Glue vellum to back side of frame, allowing excess paper to go past edges. Trim paper with razor blade. Lightly mist paper with an atomizer. The moisture causes the vellum to shrink and become tight. Measure the depth of the top of the window frame. Cut a rail the length of the window frame. It must be deep enough to attach with wood screws to the top of the window frame and also accommodate the track that holds the screens. Attach the track to the rail, according to directions. Attach hardware to screens and hang in track.

FABRIC-STRIPED PILLOWS
(PICTURED ON PAGE 27)
- **Cut two fabric rectangles,** measuring 12×24 inches. Cut one contrasting stripe, 5×12 inches. Press ¼-inch hems on the long sides of stripe. Cut a thin piece of batting ½ inch narrower than the stripe. Center batting on the pillow front. Center stripe over batting and stitch fabric into place. With right sides facing, sew pillow front to back, leaving an opening for turning and stuffing. Turn pillow right side out, fill with fiberfill stuffing or pillow form, and sew opening closed.

NURSERY CORNICE
SKILL LEVEL
Advanced
TIME (WITH CONSTRUCTION, PAINTING, AND INSTALLATION)
2 days
SUPPLIES
- ½-inch plywood cut to fit
- Sandpaper
- Finishing nails
- Screws
- Paint

PAINTED CRIB
SKILL LEVEL
Beginner
TIME (WITH DRYING TIME)
2 days
SUPPLIES
- Second-time-around crib
- Nontoxic, enamel paint (spray or can)
- Primer
- Sandpaper
- Tack cloth
- Brushes
- Accent paint colors if desired

NURSERY CORNICE
(PICTURED ON PAGES **94–95**)

■ **The size of the cornice depends on the window width and configuration.** In this project, the top of the cornice rests on, and is attached with screws to, the window frame. When you measure to calculate cornice size, remember the cornice should be tall enough to cover any drapery rods or hardware. The width can be wider than the window frame, depending on how much wall you would like to be covered with drapery. The cornice should also be deep enough to accommodate the space needed for hardware and drapery. Here, the cornice was painted with the same paint color and pattern as the wall border. This carries the eye up and connects the cornice to the rest of the room.

PAINTED CRIB
(PICTURED ON PAGE **95**)

■ **If you are planning to use an older crib,** make sure all the parts are present and the crib meets current safety standards. For safety, slats should never be more than 2⅜ inches apart. Never use a crib with missing or unsafe parts. Before painting, sand the bed to roughen the surfaces so paint will adhere. Wipe off dust with tack cloths and/or clean, damp rags. Prime the surfaces. Allow to dry. Paint with a good quality, durable enamel appropriate for infant furniture. Spray or brush on depending on paint. Highlight the bed with additional accent colors if desired.

COLORWASHED GINGHAM WALL
SKILL LEVEL
Advanced
TIME (INCLUDING DRYING AND TAPING)
2 to 3 days
SUPPLIES
- 5 pastel colors of latex paint (1 quart each; satin finish)
- Off-white latex paint (1 gallon; satin finish)
- Straightedge with level
- Colored pencils
- Low tack painter's tape
- Water-based decorator's glaze
- 5 plastic buckets with lids
- Paint tray and liner
- Paint roller
- Brush
- Stencil adhesive or tape
- Stencil roller

COLORWASHED GINGHAM WALL
(PICTURED ON PAGES 94–95)

- **Choose five pastel colors** for the colorwashes. Here, the plaid band is painted light blue, dark blue, and peachy pink. The upper portion of the wall is painted light yellow, the lower portion in stripes of pastel green and pastel turquoise.
- **Prepare the room.** Begin by painting the entire room off-white. Allow paint to dry. Measure 44 inches up from the floor and draw a horizontal line around the room. Use a level and a colored pencil that matches one of the colorwashes to mark your horizontal line.
- **Working from the bottom of your wall** up to the horizontal line, mark off 10-inch stripes, using the level, a colored pencil, and the low tack painter's tape. Rub the tape with the back of a spoon to prevent the colorwashes from bleeding under your tape. The stripes will be painted after the gingham band is completed. Apply tape around the room beneath the marked horizontal line.
- **Mix the colorwashes** in a 4:1 ratio, glaze to paint. Prepare the yellow colorwash first. Pour it into a paint tray, then roll the color onto the upper portion of the wall.
- **You may find it easier to work with a partner** when painting the gingham band. Pour glaze into a paint tray and have your partner roll on the glaze while you follow with a brush and "brush out" the glaze. Be sure to cut in the edges with your brush. Try to be consistent and work one wall at a time. Finish the entire wall without stopping. Have your partner roll two vertical rolls,

then brush them out and have your partner roll two more vertical rolls, etc. Move quickly.
- **If you do not have a partner,** fill a small container with glaze. Brush the glaze onto the wall, moving as quickly as possible. Cut in your edges as you go, then brush them out.
- **Choose a commercial stencil pattern** for a gingham look. The gingham stencil for this project has three overlays. Follow the directions on the stencil package. Tape the stencil into place, per instructions. The horizontal lines go on first with a stencil roller. For this project, first apply the darker blue colorwash. Next, apply the peachy pink horizontal lines. To complete, apply the light blue vertical lines. After the stenciled border is completed, touch up with a small brush as needed. You may find it is necessary to hand-paint and cut overlays to reach tight corners.
- **After you complete the gingham,** draw 10-inch vertical lines that extend from the bottom of the gingham to the floor. Use your level and a colored pencil that is close to the color the stripes will be glazed. Next, tape off every other vertical stripe, pressing down the tape with the back of a spoon and colorwash first one color (pastel green), then remove the tape and allow to dry. Then tape off the other stripes and colorwash the next color (pastel turquoise). If you do not want to tape off the sections, simply hand-paint each section with a tapered trimming brush. Whichever technique you use, be sure to "brush out" all of the strokes to give a more uniform texture.

DO-IT-YOURSELF LUXURY RESORT-STYLE BED
SKILL LEVEL
Beginners
TIME
30 minutes
SUPPLIES
- Dust ruffle
- Mattress pad
- Feather mattress
- Flat and fitted sheets
- Blanket
- Pillow cases and pillow shams
- Coverlet or duvet
- Iron

DO-IT-YOURSELF LUXURY RESORT-STYLE BED
■ **Treat your guests**—or yourself—to the luxury of the ultimate comfortable bed. Here's how some of the best-known inns and nicest bed-and-breakfasts pamper their guests:

■ **Make sure your mattress and box springs are in good condition.** If your set is more than five years old, consider purchasing a new one. To make the bed, remove the mattress and cover the springs with a dust ruffle if you are using one. Cover the mattress with a quality, quilted mattress pad. For extra comfort, top with a feather-bed cover from a linen shop, outlet, or specialty catalog. (If you are allergic to feathers, purchase a synthetic, fiber-filled cover.)

■ **Shop for all-cotton sheets for the longest wear and most comfort.** Sheets are sold by thread count. The higher the thread count, the softer and more luxurious the sheet. Sheets with at least a 300 thread count are considered luxury quality. However, good quality all-cotton sheets are sold in 200-plus thread counts. (**A**) Make the bed by covering the feather bed with the fitted bottom sheet. (**B**) Add a top sheet, then a thin wool, synthetic, or cotton blanket. Top with a second flat sheet as illustrated to neatly encase the blanket in two sheets. (**C**) Double-case at least four pillows or two pillows and two throw pillows to finish your bed in style and comfort. (**D**) Depending on the season and preference, finish with a coverlet or a duvet inside a duvet cover.

HELPFUL HINT
■ **Ironing all-cotton sheets is a chore.** But ironing pillow cases and the top hems of the flat sheets imparts a feel of luxury with only a little extra work. **See page 112 for linen source.**

CONTRIBUTORS/RESOURCES

Pages 12-15 Project design and styling: Wade Scherrer, Des Moines, Iowa; fabric: Country Life toile de Jouy, courtesy of Waverly Fabrics, 800/423-5881; www.waverly.com for retail locations; decorative painting: Patricia Mohr Krarmer, Ames, Iowa; slipcover design and fabrication: Sonja Carmon, photography: King Au/Studio Au, Des Moines, Iowa.

Pages 16-17 Design: Cheri Brichetto, Jennifer McLellan, Rita Peltz, Imaginations, Des Moines, Iowa; Photo styling: Wade Scherrer; photography: Greg Scheideman, Des Moines, Iowa: Butler House on Grand (bed and breakfast), Des Moines, Iowa.

Pages 22-23 Regional editor: Mary Baskin, Waco, Texas; photography: Jenifer Jordan, Waxahatchie, Texas.

Pages 26-27 Project design and styling: Wade Scherrer; photography: King Au/Studio Au; source for elastic webbing: King Textiles, Toronto, Canada, 416/504-0600.

Pages 34-35 Regional editor: Mary Baskin; photography: Jenifer Jordan.

Pages 36-37 Project design and styling: Wade Scherrer, photography: King Au/Studio Au.

Pages 54-55 Design: Terie Fletcher, Aimie Jackman, Veronica Fisher-Tewell, C'est La Vie, West Des Moines, Iowa; photography: Greg Scheideman; location: Butler House on Grand.

Page 66 Design: Victoria Veiock and Linda Moon, Wicker and the Works, West Des Moines, Iowa; photo styling: Wade Scherrer; photography: Greg Scheideman.

Pages 80-81 Bed: Murphy Beds & Custom Cabinets, 7550 Miramar Road, Suite 400, San Diego, CA 92126.

Pages 90-91 Design, Sally Draughon, Previews, Macon, Georgia; photography: Emily Minton, Atlanta; Waverly Fabics, 800/423-5881; www.waverly.com.

Pages 94-95 Project design and styling: Patricia Kramer; photography: Studio Au.

Pages 96-97 Project design, Sally Draughon; photography: Emily Minton; Waverly Fabics.

Pages 102-111: Photography: Studio Au.

Page 111 Styling: Wade Scherrer; linens: Peacock Alley, Prelude, courtesy of Holub Key Ltd., 4163 109th St, Urbandale, Iowa 50322; 515/254-1744.

U.S. UNITS TO METRIC EQUIVALENTS

To Convert From	Multiply By	To Get
Inches	25.4	Millimeters (mm)
Inches	2.54	Centimeters (cm)
Feet	30.48	Centimeters (cm)
Feet	0.3048	Meters (m)

METRIC UNITS TO U.S. EQUIVALENTS

To Convert From	Multiply By	To Get
Millimeters	0.0394	Inches
Centimeters	0.3937	Inches
Centimeters	0.0328	Feet
Meters	3.2808	Feet